U0027861

The

BOOK

of

ANSWERS

解答之書

專屬於你的人生答案

卡羅・波特
CAROL BOLT

HOW TO USE
THE BOOK OF ANSWERS

本書使用方法

❖

1. 把本書放在腿上或是桌上。

2. 提問問題時，要用「封閉式問題」陳述，並花 10 ～ 15 秒
   默想。例如：「我現在應徵的工作適合我嗎？」「這週末
   該出去旅遊嗎？」

3. 詢問時，請放把手放在封面上，並在書緣來回移動。

4. 當你覺得是時候了，按著感動翻開，就是《解答之書》
   給你的答案。

5. 每問一個問題都要比照此流程。

YOU WILL NOT BE DISAPPOINTED

————•◆•————

你不會失望的

SAVE IT FOR ANOTHER TIME

——— •♦• ———

留待下次再說

YOUR ACTIONS
WILL IMPROVE THINGS

採取行動，事情就會有轉機

DON'T BET ON IT

———◆◆———

這事大概沒譜

ADOPT AN ADVENTUROUS ATTITUDE

採取冒險的心態

FOLLOW THE ADVICE OF EXPERTS

———◆◆◆———

遵循專家的建議

YOU COULD FIND YOURSELF
UNABLE TO COMPROMISE

———•••———

你可能會發現自己無法將就

FOCUS ON YOUR HOME LIFE

專注在你的家庭生活

INVESTIGATE AND THEN ENJOY IT

———◆◆◆———

找一件事，
認真專研它並且享受其中。

DEFINITELY

---···---

當然！還用說嗎？

ONLY DO IT ONCE

————— ••• —————

只此一次

YOU MAY HAVE OPPOSITION

———•••———

你可能會遇上反對

GENTLE PERSISTENCE WILL PAY OFF

———— ••• ————

溫和的堅持會有回報

IT WILL REMAIN UNPREDICTABLE

————— ••• —————

目前還難以預測

YOU'LL NEED TO
TAKE THE INITIATIVE

————— •••• —————

你需要採取主動

CONSIDER IT AN OPPORTUNITY

———•••———

把它當成是個機會吧！

BE DELIBERATE

———◆◆◆———

深思熟慮，刻意為之

ABSOLUTELY NOT

———— ••• ————

絕對不可以！

EXPLORE IT
WITH PLAYFUL CURIOSITY

————◆◆◆————

用好奇玩心多加探索

PERHAPS, WHEN YOU'RE OLDER

—— ◆◆◆ ——

你再老一點的話 …… 有可能喔！

BE DELIGHTFULLY SURE OF IT

———•••———

快快樂樂地信心滿滿

BETTER TO WAIT

———◆◆◆———

最好等等

REPRIORITIZE WHAT IS IMPORTANT

—◆◆—

重新按照事情重要性排列

IT SEEMS ASSURED

———◆———

看起來滿穩的

CREATE MORE SPACE FOR IT

多創造出一些空間吧！

DO IT EARLY

————— ✦ —————

及早開始

KEEP IT TO YOURSELF

———◆◆———

有些事自己知道就好

ALLOW YOURSELF TO REST FIRST

———•••———

允許自己先好好休息

MAKE YOURSELF USEFUL

————— •‡• —————

當個有用一點的人好嗎？

YOU'LL HAVE TO
MAKE IT UP AS YOU GO

——— ◆◆◆ ———

走一步，算一步

STARTLING EVENTS
MAY OCCUR AS A RESULT

———•◦•———

結果可能會讓你驚到下巴掉下來哦！

THE ANSWER MAY COME TO YOU IN ANOTHER LANGUAGE

解答會到來，只是可能不是說中文

TRY A MORE UNLIKELY SOLUTION

———◆◆◆———

試試天馬行空的方法

YOU WILL NEED TO ACCOMMODATE

———◆◆◆———

你得配合環境行事

DOUBT IT

——◆◆◆——

懷疑是種美德

CAST YOUR NET WIDER

———•••———

多試試才知道

IT WILL BRING GOOD LUCK

———— ◆◆◆ ————

這會帶來好運

IT MAY BE DIFFICULT
BUT YOU WILL FIND VALUE IN IT

———••——

此事難雖難，其中有價值

BE PATIENT

———— ✦ ————

有點耐心嘛！

YOU WILL FIND OUT EVERYTHING YOU'LL NEED TO KNOW

你會得到需要知道的一切

❦

THERE IS A SUBSTANTIAL LINK TO ANOTHER SITUATION

———— ••• ————

這和另一情況之間有著重大關連

WATCH AND SEE WHAT HAPPENS

———•••———

等著看會發生什麼事

YOU KNOW BETTER NOW
THAN EVER BEFORE

———•••———

你現在明辨是非的能力前所未有地好

IT WILL AFFECT
HOW OTHERS SEE YOU

————•••————

這會影響別人對你的看法

RECONSIDER YOUR APPROACH

---•••---

重新考慮你採取的方法

YOU'LL BE HAPPY YOU DID

———◆◆———

你會很開心自己這麼做了

GET IT IN WRITING

———•••———

白紙黑字才不會忘

UNFAVORABLE AT THIS TIME

———•••———

此時不宜

IT IS NOT SOMETHING TO BE TAKEN LIGHTLY

——◆◆——

此事不宜等閒視之

UPGRADE ANY WAY YOU CAN

———◆———

想盡各種辦法提升自己吧！

IF YOU DO AS YOU'RE TOLD

———— ✦ ————

別人怎麼說，你就怎麼做

IF IT IS DONE WELL;
IF NOT, DON'T DO IT AT ALL

---◆---

要做就好好做，不然乾脆就別做

DON'T ASK FOR ANY MORE
AT THIS TIME

———— ·•· ————

目前就先別再要求更多了

DON'T BE RIDICULOUS

———◆———

別鬧了

AVOID THE FIRST SOLUTION

—•••—

別選近在眼前的解決方案

YOU'LL GET THE FINAL WORD

———◆◆◆———

你說了算

PROCEED AT A MORE RELAXED PACE

———————

用更輕鬆的步調進行吧！

THE BEST SOLUTION MAY NOT BE THE OBVIOUS ONE

最明顯的方法不見得最好

REMAIN FLEXIBLE

————— •◦• —————

保持彈性

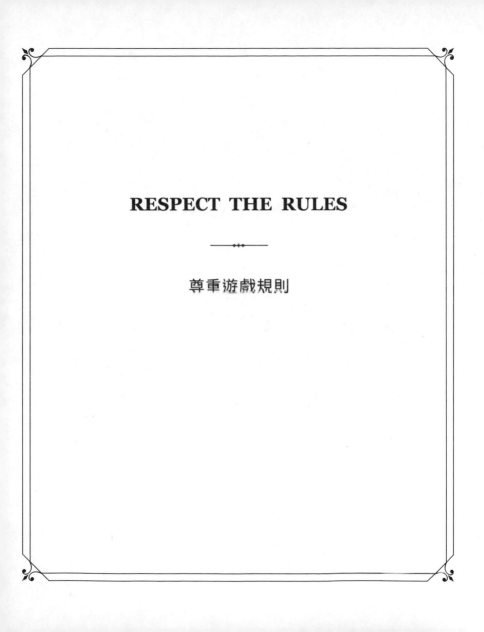

RESPECT THE RULES

尊重游戲規則

TAKE THE LEAD

———◆◆———

當領頭羊吧！

CHOOSE YOUR WORDS CAREFULLY

———◆◆———

小心選擇用字

YOU MAY BE HANGING ONTO
AN OUTDATED IDEAL

———◆———

你死抓的概念可能有點過時了喔！

THERE MAY BE A STRUGGLE

———— ••• ————

可能會是一場硬戰

YOU'LL NEED A LITTLE MORE ENTHUSIASM

你需要多點熱情

THAT'S OUT OF YOUR CONTROL

————•••————

這事你已經管不著了

PROVIDED YOU SAY 'THANK YOU'

---◆---

將獲得所需的事物。記得說聲謝謝!

ENJOY THE EXPERIENCE

———◆◆———

享受過程吧！

APPROACH CAUTIOUSLY

———◆◆◆———

謹慎處理

BE YOUR OWN BEST ADVOCATE

---◆◆◆---

為自己謀取最佳利益

BE HAPPY FOR ANOTHER

———✦———

為別人開心

PAY ATTENTION TO THE DETAILS

留意細節

WATCH YOUR STEP AS YOU GO

————•••————

小心每一步

SPEAK UP ABOUT IT

———◆◆———

不用顧忌，大聲說出來！

DON'T HESITATE

別猶豫！

THIS IS A GOOD TIME TO MAKE A NEW PLAN

現在正是做新計畫的好時機

MOVE ON

是時候向前走了

DON'T WASTE YOUR TIME

———•••———

別浪費你的時間

A STRONG COMMITMENT
WILL ACHIEVE GOOD RESULTS

———◆◆◆———

堅定的投入會帶來好結果

IT MAY NOT BE LOGICAL

這不太合理喔！

THERE IS NO GUARANTEE

————— ••• —————

這可沒個保證

THE CIRCUMSTANCES
WILL CHANGE VERY QUICKLY

———•••———

環境很快就會有改變

DON'T GET CAUGHT UP
IN YOUR EMOTIONS

———◆———

別陷在自己的情緒裡

SHIFT YOUR FOCUS

———◆◆———

轉移焦點！

IT IS SIGNIFICANT

———•••———

這很重要

REPRIORITIZE WHAT IS IMPORTANT

———— ✦ ————

重新按照事情重要性排列

MAKE A LIST OF WHY NOT

———— ••• ————

列出「不妨一試」的理由吧！

DON'T WAIT

———•••———

麥擱等阿！

TAKE YOUR TIME

———•••———

慢慢來比較快

THERE IS A GOOD REASON
TO BE OPTIMISTIC

———◆◆———

總有保持樂觀的好理由

IT IS SOMETHING
YOU WON'T FORGET

———— •••• ————

曾讓你難以忘懷的喔！

SEEK OUT MORE OPTIONS

———◦◦◦———

多找幾個選項

FOLLOW THROUGH
ON YOUR OBLIGATIONS

————— ••• —————

該完成的事請徹底完成

DEAL WITH IT LATER

---◆◆◆---

晚點再處理

REVEAL YOUR THOUGHTS
TO A TRUSTED CONFIDANTE

———◆◆———

找閨蜜／紅粉知己說說真正的想法

FOLLOW SOMEONE ELSE'S LEAD

———— ••• ————

跟隨別人的帶領

YOU COULD FIND YOURSELF
UNABLE TO COMPROMISE

————◆◆◆————

你可能會發現自己無法將就

MAKE A LIST OF WHY

列出「這麼做」的理由吧！

DON'T BE PRESSURED
INTO ACTING TOO QUICKLY

———◆◆———

別因為壓力而太快行動

TAKE A CHANCE

———◆◆———

不妨一試！

YOUR ACTIONS
WILL IMPROVE THINGS

———•••———

採取行動，事情就會有轉機

ASK FOR HELP

———·⁜·———

請人幫忙

KNOW WHEN IT'S TIME TO GO

———————

要知道何時該放手

ACCEPT A CHANGE TO
YOUR ROUTINE

———◆◆———

在日常習慣中做一個改變

YOU'LL NEED TO
TAKE THE INITIATIVE

———— •••• ————

你需要採取主動

YOU'LL HAVE TO COMPROMISE

——◆◆——

你得妥協

YOU NEED MORE INFORMATION

———◆◆◆———

你需要更多資訊

TRUST YOUR ORIGINAL THOUGHT

———·••·———

相信自己最一開始的想法

SEEK OUT THE PATH OF
LEAST RESISTANCE

———— •••• ————

請去找一條阻力最小的路走吧！

IT WILL CREATE A STIR

———•••———

這會造成一些混亂

REMOVE YOUR OWN OBSTACLES

———❖❖———

處理掉那些會扯自己後腿的事

IT WOULD BE BETTER
TO FOCUS ON YOUR WORK

———•••———

還是專注在自己的工作上就好

IT WILL BE A PLEASURE

————•••————

那可是你的榮幸呢！

BE MORE GENEROUS

大方一點！

BET ON IT

——— ✦ ———

賭一把吧！

GOOD THINGS
ARE SEEKING YOUR OUT

———•••———

好事即將來叩門！

DON'T LEAVE ROOM FOR REGRET

——•••——

別給遺憾留空間

MAKE A CONTRIBUTION

---◆◆◆---

有點貢獻好嗎？

MISHAPS ARE HIGHLY PROBABLE

———— ✦ ————

高度注意！很可能遭遇不幸事件！

PRESS FOR CLOSURE

———

全力進攻，讓這事能畫上句點

REALIZE THAT TOO MANY CHOICES IS AS DIFFICULT AS TOO FEW

———•••———

要知道：太多或太少選擇都一樣難搞

YES

———◆◆◆———

沒錯！

YOU ARE SURE TO HAVE SUPPORT

---◆---

你一定會獲得支持

LISTEN CAREFULLY;
THEN YOU WILL KNOW

———◆◆◆———

仔細地聽，你就會知道！

THE ANSWER
IS IN YOUR BACKYARD

———◆◆———

答案就在你身邊

LAUGH ABOUT IT

一笑置之吧！

LET YOUR EMOTIONS GUIDE YOU

———◆◆◆———

讓你的感受引導你！

OTHERS WILL DEPEND ON YOUR CHOICES

———◆◆◆———

其他人要靠你的選擇了

LET IT GO

放下吧！

IT COULD BE A WASTE OF MONEY

---◆◆◆---

這大概又會浪費錢

IT'S TIME FOR YOU TO GO

———◆◆———

是時候該離開了

DON'T BE DISTRACTED

———✦———

别分心了！

GIVE IT ALL YOU'VE GOT

———— ••• ————

傾盡你有的一切吧！

YOU DON'T REALLY CARE

---◆---

你根本不在乎

YOU'LL NEED TO CONSIDER OTHER WAYS

————•◆•————

你得想想其他辦法了！

A YEAR FROM NOW
IT WON'T MATTER

———•••———

一年後再回頭看，這件事根本就不重要了

FOLLOW THE ADVICE OF EXPERTS

————•••————

遵循專家的建議

IT COULD BE EXTRAORDINARY

---◆---

可能會相當了不得喔！

COUNT TO 10; ASK AGAIN

———◆◆◆———

數到十，然後再問一次

ACT AS THOUGH
IT IS ALREADY REAL

———◆———

以已經實現了的態度行動吧！

SETTING PRIORITIES WILL BE A NECESSARY PART OF THE PROCESS

——— •‡• ———

排定優先順序，是過程中必要的一環

USE YOUR IMAGINATION

———•••———

發揮想像力！

IT'S GONNA BE GREAT

——＋＋——

事情會很順利

TO ENSURE THE BEST DECISION, BE CALM

為了確保這是最好的決定，要冷靜！

WAIT

———•••———

先等等 I

YOU'LL HAVE TO MAKE IT UP
AS YOU GO

———◆———

走一步，算一步

FOLLOW THE DIRECTIONS

—— •••• ——

順著走下去就對了！

EXPECT TO SETTLE

———•••———

準備安定下來

UNQUESTIONABLY

———— ✦ ————

毫無疑問

OF COURSE

——◆◆◆——

當然啦！

LOOK FOR WHAT MAY BE HIDDEN

———◆◆◆———

找找看還有什麼隱藏的事物

YOU KNOW BETTER NOW
THAN EVER BEFORE

———◆◆◆———

你現在明辨是非的能力前所未有地好

TRUST YOUR INTUITION

———◆◆———

相信你的直覺

DON'T MISS AN OPPORTUNITY

———◆◆———

機會出現別錯過

ASK YOUR FATHER

———•••———

去問你爸

ASK YOUR MOTHER

去問你媽

PERHAPS, WHEN YOU'RE OLDER

你再老一點的話 …… 有可能喔！

MAYBE

---◆◆---

可能喔！

FINISH SOMETHING ELSE FIRST

———•••———

先去做其他事

YOU MAY HAVE OPPOSITION

———•••———

你可能會遇上反對

YOU ARE TOO CLOSE TO SEE

———•••———

你靠太近了，所以看不清楚

THE SITUATION IS UNCLEAR

現在情況還不明朗

A SUBSTANTIAL EFFORT
WILL BE REQUIRED

———•••———

你得付出相當的努力

ALLOW YOURSELF TO REST FIRST

---◆◆◆---

允許自己先好好休息

THE CHANCE
WILL NOT COME AGAIN SOON

————•◆•————

如此良機近日將不再有

THE ANSWER MAY COME TO YOU IN ANOTHER LANGUAGE

—◆◆—

解答會到來，只是可能不是說中文

RECONSIDER YOUR APPROACH

———◆◆———

重新考慮你採取的方法

IT WOULD BE INADVISABLE

———— ••• ————

這不可取！

THERE IS A SMALL PRICE TO PAY

---◆◆---

要付點小小代價了

WAIT FOR A BETTER OFFER

——— •••• ———

等待更好的提案

SETTLE IT SOON

———•••———

趕快搞定

REMAIN OBJECTIVE

---◆---

請保持客觀

YES, BUT DON'T FORCE IT

———— ••• ————

是的，但別硬來

GET A CLEARER VIEW

---◆---

換個更清楚的觀點

BE DELIGHTFULLY SURE OF IT

———•••———

快快樂樂地信心滿滿

NOW YOU CAN

———✦✦✦———

現在可以

PROVIDED YOU SAY 'THANK YOU'

———◆◆◆———

將獲得所需的事物。記得說聲謝謝！

DON'T OVERDO IT

————◆◆◆————

別畫蛇添足啊！

IT WILL SUSTAIN YOU

———•••———

救兵會出現

IT COULD COST YOU

---•‡•---

這可能會讓你付出代價

ADOPT AN ADVENTUROUS ATTITUDE

—— •+• ——

採取冒險的心態

IT IS SURE
TO MAKE THINGS INTERESTING

———◆◆———

這當然會讓事情更有趣

BE PRACTICAL

———•••———

實際點！

ARE YOU READY?

———•••———

你準備好了嗎？

SAVE YOUR ENERGY

———◆◆◆———

省省力氣吧！

PAY ATTENTION TO THE DETAILS

———•••———

留意細節！

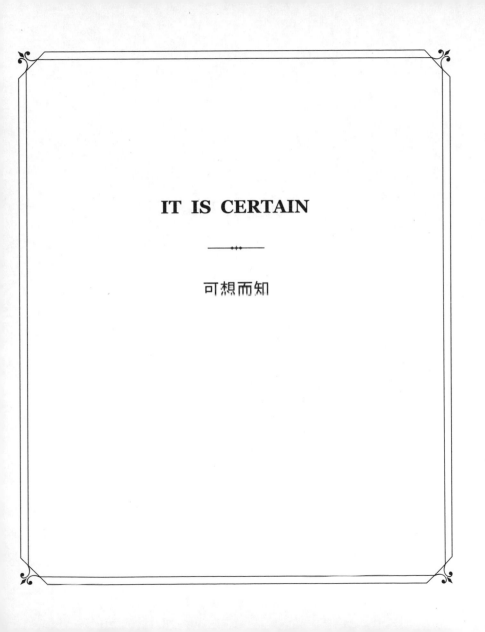

IT IS CERTAIN

可想而知

IT IS UNCERTAIN

———— ✦ ————

還無法確定

THE OUTCOME WILL BE POSITIVE

—— •••• ——

一定有正面的結果

YOU MAY HAVE TO DROP
OTHER THINGS

———•‖•———

你或許得放下其他事

DON'T BE CONCERNED

---◆◆---

別憂心！

PREPARE FOR THE UNEXPECTED

準備好，將有意外之事發生

IT IS NOT SIGNIFICANT

———◆◆◆———

這沒意義

TELL SOMEONE
WHAT IT MEANS TO YOU

———◆◆◆———

告訴某人這對你的意義何在

WHATEVER YOU DO
THE RESULTS WILL BE LASTING

———◦•◦———

不管做什麼，成果都能保持下去

KEEP AN OPEN MIND

————•••————

保持開放心態

IT'S A GOOD TIME TO MAKE PLANS

———•••———

現在是計畫的好時機！

IT MAY BE DIFFICULT
BUT YOU WILL FIND VALUE IN IT

———•••———

此事雖難，其中有價值

IT IS WORTH THE TROUBLE

———— ••• ————

這點麻煩值得的！

THERE WILL BE
OBSTACLES TO OVERCOME

———— •••• ————

會遇到需要克服的困難

RELATED ISSUES MAY SURFACE

———◆◆◆———

相關問題將會浮上檯面

YOU ARE SURE TO HAVE SUUPORT

———•••———

你一定會獲得支持

IT MAY BE UNCOMFORTABLE

這可能不會太舒服

ASSISTANCE WOULD MAKE YOUR PROGRESS A SUCCESS

成功就是需要一點協助

COLLABORATION WILL BE THE KEY

—•••—

合作是關鍵

SEEK OUT MORE OPTIONS

多找幾個選項

TAKE CHARGE

掌握住局面！

IT CANNOT FAIL

———◆◆———

這不可能失敗的！

YOU MUST ACT NOW

———◆———

現！在！就！行！動！

RESPECT THE RULES

———◆◆———

尊重規則

GENTLE PERSISTENCE WILL PAY OFF

———— ◆◆ ————

溫和堅持會有回報

YOU COULD BE DISAPPOINTED

———◆◆◆———

你可能會失望

IT MAY ALREADY BE A DONE DEAL

———◆◆◆———

木已成舟

FOLLOW THROUGH
WITH YOUR GOOD INTENTIONS

———◆———

帶著善意完成使命

TAKE MORE TIME TO DECIDE

---❖---

多花些時間想想再決定

FOLLOW THROUGH
ON YOUR OBLIGATIONS

———— ••• ————

該完成的事請徹底完成

DON'T BE PRESSURED
INTO ACTING TOO QUICKLY

---••---

別因為有壓力而太快行動

DON'T IGNORE THE OBVIOUS

---◆◆◆---

不要忽視那最明顯的

OTHERS WILL DEPEND ON YOUR CHOICES

———•••———

很多人都仰賴你的決定

DON'T BE TOO PRACTICAL

———— ⊁⊰ ————

不要太實際

BE A GOOD ROLE MODEL

—•••—

做一個好典範

IT'S NOT WORTH A STRUGGLE

———— ◆◆ ————

這不值得你苦苦掙扎．

LISTEN CAREFULLY;
THEN YOU WILL KNOW

———◆◆◆———

仔細地聽，你就會知道！

DON'T FORGET TO HAVE FUN

———•◆•———

別忘了要開心

DON'T DOUBT IT

———◆◆◆———

别懷疑！

A STRONG COMMITMENT
WILL ACHIEVE GOOD RESULTS

——◆◆◆——

堅定的投入會帶來好結果

TRY A MORE UNLIKELY SOLUTION

———•••———

試試天馬行空的方法

LEAVE BEHIND OLD SOLUTIONS

—·••·—

丟掉舊方法

KEEP IT TO YOURSELF

———— •••• ————

有些事自己知道就好

WATCH YOUR STEP AS YOU GO

———⋅⋅———

小心每一步

EXPLORE IT
WITH PLAYFUL CURIOSITY

—◆—

用好奇坑心多加探索

DON'T BE TOO DEMANDING

———◆◆◆———

別過度苛求

DON'T LEAVE ROOM FOR REGRET

---◆◆◆---

別給遺憾留空間

ACT AS THOUGH
IT IS ALREADY REAL

———— •••• ————

以已經實現了的態度行動吧！

IT ISN'T PERSONAL

———•••———

並非針對你

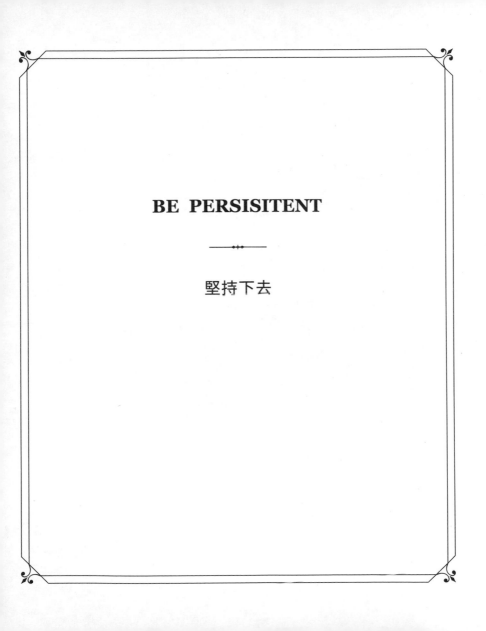

BE PERSISITENT

堅持下去

CHOOSE WHAT WILL
MAKE YOU HAPPY

———— •••• ————

選會讓自己開心的

DON'T LET MONEY DECIDE IT

——— ✦ ———

不要用錢當做決定的條件

IT WILL WORK ITSELF OUT

———— ••• ————

生命會自己找到出路

IF IT'S TOO DIFFICULT, MAYBE IT'S NOT YOURS

———◆◆———

如果太過困難，表示它可能不屬於你

IT COULD MEAN THAT
YOU MAY HAVE TO DO SOMETHING
THAT YOU'VE NEVER DONE

———•••———

這可能表示你得去做不曾做過的事！

DECIDE WHERE YOU WANT TO BE
AND HEAD IN THAT DIRECTION

———◆◆———

先決定你想去哪，然後就朝它的方向前進吧！

CAST YOUR NET WIDER

———•••———

多試試才知道

MAKE NO ASSUMPTIONS

別預設立場

RESPECT THE FUNDAMENTALS

—•••—

不要小看基礎

MAKE YOURSELF USEFUL

—— ✦ ——

當個有用一點的人好嗎？

FIND MORE TIME

擠出更多時間

NOTHING WILL COMPARE

———◆◆◆———

沒有任何事比得上

IT WILL BE AN OPPORTUNITY

———

這會是個機會

DON'T GIVE UP YOUR RIGHT TO WAIT

---◆◆◆---

等待是權利，別輕易放棄

BE DELIBERATE

———◆◆◆———

深思熟慮，刻意為之

WHY IS IT IMPORTANT TO YOU?

這為什麼對你很重要？

DON'T LET THE MOMENT PASS

---◆◆◆---

別錯失這個瞬間

YOU'LL GET WHAT YOU SETTLE FOR

———◆◆◆———

一旦妥協，你就不會得到更好的了

CHOOSE WHATEVER
WILL HELP YOU TO GROW

———◆◆———

選擇能讓你成長的事物

BE KIND

———•••———

當個和善的人

REALIZE THAT TOO MANY CHOICES IS AS DIFFICULT AS TOO FEW

——◆◆——

要知道：太多或太少選擇都一樣難搞

TAKE A CHANCE

不妨一試！

❧

OTHERS MAY NOT APPROVE

———◆◆◆———

其他人不見得會贊同

YOU'LL NEED A LITTLE MORE ENTHUSIASM

---◆◆◆---

你需要多一點熱情

INITIATE AN ADVENTURE

———◆◆◆———

發動一場冒險吧！

BE TACTFUL

機靈點

YOU'LL NEED TO
CONSIDER OTHER WAYS

————•••————

你得想想其他辦法了！

FIGURE OUT A WAY

想出辦法來！

IT COULD BE A MATTER OF PRIDE

———◆———

這事關面子！

PURSURE MORE VARIETY

———◆◆◆———

尋求多種可能

DON'T GET CAUGHT UP IN YOUR EMOTIONS

---◆◆◆---

別陷在自己的情緒裡

PITCH IN WHATEVER YOU CAN

---◆◆---

多少幫點忙吧！

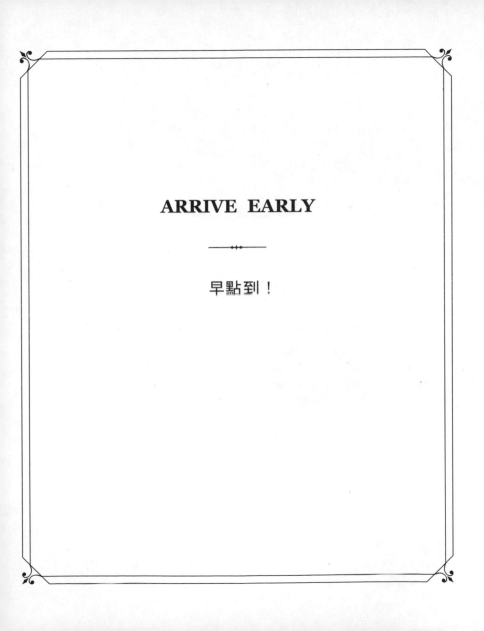

ARRIVE EARLY

———◆◆◆———

早點到！

NO MATTER WHAT

——◆——

無論如何

YOU ARE TOO CLOSE TO SEE

————◆◆◆————

你靠太近了，所以看不清楚

YES

———✦———

沒錯！

DON'T TAKE A CHANCE

———◆◆◆———

別冒險一試

IT IS NOT SOMETHING TO BE
TAKEN LIGHTLY

———◆◆———

此事不宜等閒視之

BE CONTENT TO LEAVE WELL ENOUGH ALONE

————•••————

現在這樣就很好了！

TOO MUCH ATTENTION
IS ON THE DETAILS

———•••———

花太多精力在細節上了

KEEP IT LIGHT

——◆◆——

輕鬆以對囉！

GET MORE SLEEP

---◆◆---

多睡點

RECONSIDER ANOTHER POSSIBILITY

———◆◆———

重新考慮其他的可能性吧！

IT MAY NOT BE LOGICAL

———•••———

這不太合理喔！

THE ANSWER IS
IN YOUR BACKYARD

---◆◆◆---

答案就在你身邊

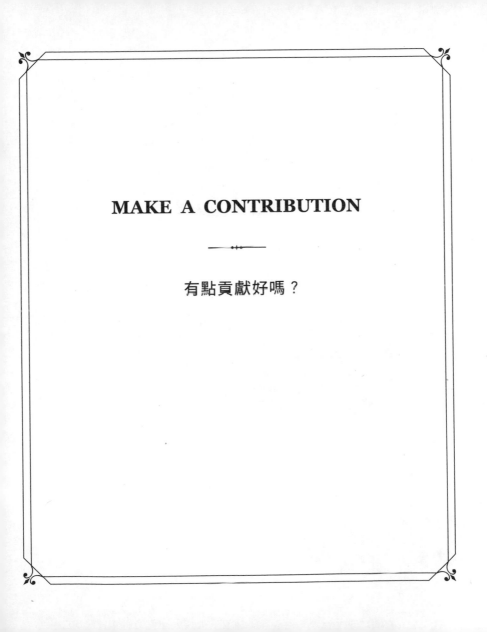

MAKE A CONTRIBUTION

有點貢獻好嗎？

USE YOUR IMAGINATION

———◆◆———

發揮想像力！

KNOW NO LIMITATIONS

——◆——

不要被限制！

BUILD SOMETHING BIGGER

———— •ı• ————

試著做更大的事

AIM HIGHER

———◆———

設立更高的目標

DON'T OVEREACT

————◦✦◦————

別過度反應了

BE A GOOD SPORT

有點風度吧！

TAKE THE LEAD

---◆---

當領頭羊吧！

THERE IS A SMALL PRICE TO PAY

要付點小小代價了

DON'T BE TOO CRITICAL

———◆◆———

别太吹毛求疵

PUT YOUR FEELINGS IN
THE RIGHT PLACE

———◆◆———

情緒要用在對的地方

IDENTIFY WHAT MATTERS ABOUT IT

—— ••• ——

找出真正重要的事

HOW THINGS TURN OUT WILL DEPEND ON YOU

事情會怎麼發展，全看你了

LOOK FOR WHAT MAY BE HIDDEN

找找看還有什麼隱藏的事物

LET YOUR EMOTIONS GUIDE YOU

――――・＋・――――

讓你的感受引導你！

REAVEAL YOUR THOUGHTS
TO A TRUSTED CONFIDANTE

———◆◆◆———

找閨密／紅粉知己說說真正的想法

TAKE A CLOSER LOOK

———·••·———

看仔細點

꧁꧂

DON'T BE CONCERNED

———◆◆◆———

別憂心！

YOU MAY HAVE TO DO THIS ON YOUR OWN

---••---

你可能得自己來了

ASK FOR HELP

請人幫忙

CREATE MORE SPACE FOR IT

— ••• —

多創造出一些空間吧!

DIVERT YOUR ATTENTION

分散你的注意力

WHAT DO YOU WANT?

———◆◆◆———

你想要什麼？

DO YOUR BEST TO STEER
OUT OF THE WAY

———◆◆———

盡全力避開任何障礙

THERE IS A GOOD REASON
TO BE OPTIMISTIC

總有保持樂觀的好理由

DON'T BE DISTRACTED

———◆◆———

别分心了！

ENJOY A NEW SETTING

———◆◆———

享受新的環境

YOU WILL NEED TO ACCOMMODATE

———•••———

你得配合環境行事

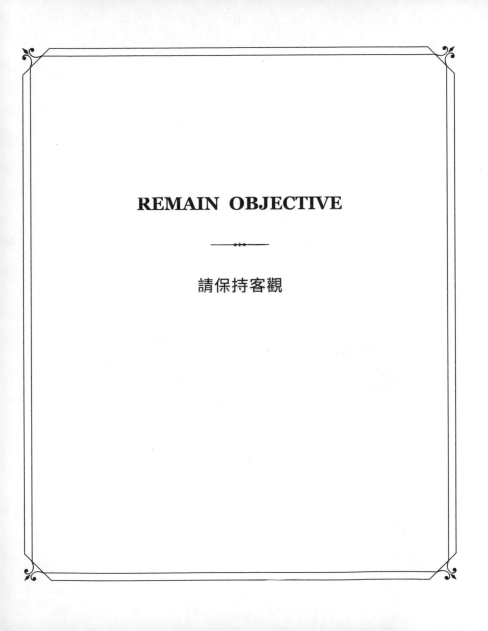

REMAIN OBJECTIVE

請保持客觀

TELL SOMEONE WHAT IT MEANS TO YOU

———•••———

告訴某人這對你的意義何在

CONSIDER IT AN OPPORTUNITY

———◆◆◆———

把它當成是個機會吧！

SEEK OUT THE ROUTE OF LEAST RESISTANCE

請去找一條阻力最小的路走吧！

GOOD THINGS
ARE SEEKING YOU OUT

———◆◆◆———

好事即將來叩門！

IT WON'T MATTER WHEN YOU DO,
BUT THAT YOU DO

———◆◆———

重要的不是什麼時候做，而是你有做

YOU MAY BE HANGING ONTO AN OUTDATED IDEAL

———•••———

你死抓的想法可能有點過時了喔！

IT'LL CHANGE YOUR LUCK

---··---

這會改變你的運勢

IF YOU DON'T RESIST

———•••———

不要抗拒就會發生

FOLLOW THE DIRECTIONS

—•••—

順著走下去就對了！

THE BEST SOLUTION MAY BE THE OBVIOUS ONE

最明顯的答案或許就是最佳解答

DON'T BE TOO CAUTIOUS

———•••———

不要過分謹慎

YOU MAY REGRET IT

———— ••• ————

你可能會後悔喔！

WHY IS IT IMPORTANT TO YOU?

———◆◆◆———

這為什麼對你很重要？

CHOOSE YOUR WORDS CAREFULLY

———•••———

小心選擇用字

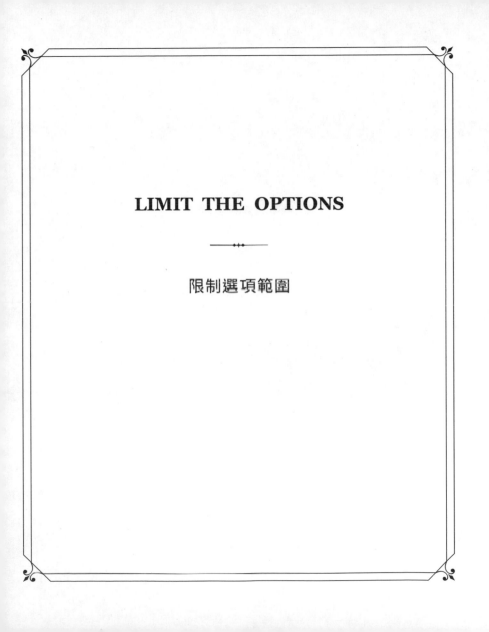

LIMIT THE OPTIONS

限制選項範圍

FOCUS YOUR ATTENTION

---◆◆◆---

集中注意力！

SHOULDN'T YOU BE OUTSIDE PLAYING?

———◆◆◆———

你不是該在外面玩耍嗎？

WOULD IT BE A PLEASURE?

———— ✦ ————

搞不好是件開心的事？

BE ON TIME

要準時喔！

ASK YOUR FATHER

———◆◆◆———

去問你爸

ASK YOUR MOTHER

去問你媽

TAKE YOUR TIME

慢慢來比較快

YES, BUT DON'T FORCE IT

———◆◆◆———

是的，但別硬來

DO YOU HAVE THE TIME?

—••—

你有這個時間嗎？

THERE IS MORE TO KNOW

---◆◆---

你要學的還多著呢！

FIND OUT THE FACTS

———— ✦ ————

找出事實

NOT IF YOU'RE ALONE

———•••———

如果你獨處，則否

UNCOVER MORE DETAILS

揭露更多細節

YOUR HEART ISN'T IN IT

———— ••• ————

你的心根本不在這

BE HAPPY FOR ANOTHER

———•+•———

為別人感到開心

YOU ARE FAVORED

---•••---

好處站在你這邊

NEVER

絕不！

A YEAR FROM NOW
IT WON'T MATTER

---◆◆---

一年後再回頭看，這件事根本就个重要了

ARE YOU READY?

你準備好了嗎?

YOU MUST

———◆◆———

你必須！

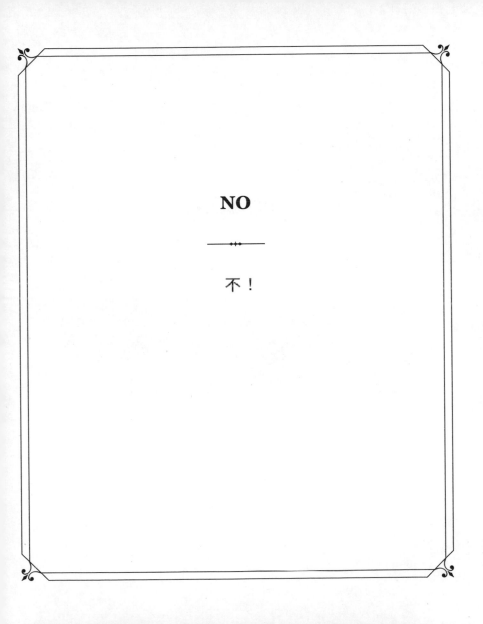

NO

不！

CONSERVE YOUR RESOURCES

有效利用資源

BE A GOOD ROLE MODEL

———— •••• ————

做一個好典範

NEGOTIATE A BETTER DEAL

———◆◆◆———

去談一個更好的條件

FAVOR THE GOOD THINGS

———•••———

喜愛美好的事物

國家圖書館出版品預行編目資料

解答之書：專屬你的人生答案 / 卡羅‧波特（Carol
Bolt）著；心心譯 . -- 臺北市：三采文化，2018.11
704 面；　公分 . --（Mindmap）
譯自：The book of answers
ISBN 978-957-658-083-3（平裝）

1. 人生哲學 2. 生活指導

191.9　　　　　　　　　　　107017907

suncolor
三采文化集團

Mind Map　172

解答之書
專屬於你的人生答案

作者｜卡羅‧波特（Carol Bolt）　　譯者｜心心
責任編輯｜朱紫綾　　美術主編｜藍秀婷　　封面內頁設計｜藍秀婷
行銷經理｜張育珊　　行銷企劃｜周傳雅　　版權負責｜杜曉涵

發行人｜張輝明　　總編輯｜曾雅青　　發行所｜三采文化股份有限公司
地址｜台北市內湖區瑞光路 513 巷 33 號 8 樓
傳訊｜TEL:8797-1234　FAX:8797-1688　　網址｜www.suncolor.com.tw
郵政劃撥｜帳號：14319060　戶名：三采文化股份有限公司
初版發行｜2018 年 11 月 30 日　定價｜NT$450
　　33刷｜2024 年 5 月 30 日